The Final-Day Book Ministry

God's Holy Word Revealed

Minister LBJ Johnson

ISBN 979-8-89130-401-7 (paperback)
ISBN 979-8-89130-402-4 (digital)

Christian Faith Publishing
832 Park Avenue
Meadville, PA 16335
www.christianfaithpublishing.com

Printed in the United States of America

The Final-Day Book Ministry

The purpose of this small easy-to-read book is to give some basic knowledge to those who are seeking a deeper spiritual relationship with God, with the hope of encouraging them to seek the full knowledge of the Holy Scriptures. The biblical revelations and knowledge in this book will also provide answers to many of the world's religious questions about the spiritual events that took place before the existence of humankind, which have never been answered. The spiritual revelations revealed in this book were revealed by the Holy Spirit of God to be taught and shared with the world. Another purpose of this book ministry is to issue the Word of God to those who do not know the Lord in the forgiveness of their sins and who are not always able to enter a physical building to hear the words of God's salvation. This small inexpensive book will teach them that the true church and the best place to reach God at any time and anywhere is in our heart and mind. Some of the world's most recent events and situations have made us realize that the possibility of attending a physical church may become out of reach or impossible at any given time. Hopefully, this book ministry will encourage readers of all ages and spiritual levels to seek the Word of God while there is still time to be saved by His Holy Spirit, because greater is the Holy Spirit that will be in you than the evil spirit that is in the world.

> You are of God, little children,
> and have overcome them: because
> greater is he that is in you, than he
> that is in the world. (1 John 4:4)

> So shall my Word be that goeth
> forth out of my mouth: it shall not
> return unto me void, but it shall
> accomplish that which I please,

and it shall prosper in the thing
whereto I sent it. (Isa. 55:11)

Heaven and earth shall pass away,
but my words shall not pass away.
(Matt. 24:35)

A MESSAGE FROM OUR LORD

Come unto me, all ye that labor and are heavy laden, and I will give you rest. Take my yoke upon you, and learn of me, for I am meek and lowly in heart and ye shall find rest unto your souls. For my yoke is easy, and my burden is light. (Matt. 11:28–30)

Come to me, all of you who are worried and in trouble, and I will give you peace. Connect yourself to me, and learn of me, because I am merciful and kindhearted, and you will find peace for your soul. Because my connections are

easy, and my ways are rewarding.
(Matt. 11:28–30 explained)

This promise of peace from our Lord and Savior Jesus Christ has been fulfilled in many lives of true believers. Believing in the Word of God and following His will and His ways are quite easy and rewarding, and this promise also comes with the gift of eternal life in the kingdom of heaven.

THE PURPOSE

For many of us, the true knowledge and understanding of the very beginning of God's existence were never fully taught or explained. As children most of us were taught that God created the heaven and the earth in six days and He rested on the seventh day, which is true, but we were not aware of some of the other events that took place between the existence of God and the completion of His creation for humankind. In these "final days," the Holy Spirit of God has revealed revelations about the beginning of existence that have never been known or taught. This new knowledge will give the world a deeper understanding of the events that took place before the creation of the earth and give answers to many biblical questions such as "*Who* is the Lord? *Why* was the heavens created? *Who* lived in the earth before mankind? *Why* was the earth filled with darkness? or *When* was the pit of hell created?"

The Lord God is a God of love and mercy, and He knows that we are not perfect because He did not create us perfect. All He asks from us is to have a spiritual relationship with Him, which consists of our belief, our prayers, and the learning of His Holy Word. Remember faith and the belief in God comes by hearing the Word of God and trusting in what you hear, but remember also that the devil wants to keep us from becoming true believers to keep us from entering the kingdom of heaven and enjoying the gift of eternal life. May the Lord add His blessings to the readers of His Word (Rom. 10:17; John 10:10).

VOLUME 1

The Existence Before Mankind

CONTENTS

CHAPTER 1

The Existence of
God the Father

God's existence is amazingly easy to understand because the complete order of all beginnings started with His powerful Holy Spirit. This powerful and almighty Spirit is also our Heavenly Father and the only true God who ever existed. Understand that our God is all-knowing, all-powerful, and all-able to do anything but fail. Know also that we will never be able to understand the knowledge of God unless we first understand the power of God. Read on to learn just how powerful our God has been forever. Before anything or anyone ever existed, our Heavenly Father existed alone as a powerful Holy Spirit, which cannot be seen, and His powerful Spirit filled the whole space of existence. What a mighty God we serve.

CHAPTER 2

The Existence of the Lord God

Then in a time beyond our knowledge, God the Father, in His infinite wisdom and power, decided to call into existence His spiritual image, whom He created just by speaking His powerful word. God created His spiritual image in the likeness of Himself. "What a mighty God we serve." God named His spiritual image *Lord*. Now there existed the Holy Spirit of God, who cannot be seen, and the spiritual image of God, who can be seen by other spiritual beings. Now because God the Heavenly Father and His image are one in the same Spirit, the Heavenly Father took on the name *The Lord God*. Knowing that His image can only be seen by spiritual eyes, the Lord God decided to create a place for His angelic image to live, so He created the kingdom of heaven. Remember the Holy Spirit of God could not be contained nor seen, but His holy image, who is the Lord of all, needed a kingdom, so the Lord God spoke the kingdom of heaven into existence. Know this the Lord God is one, and He created the world and all that ever existed (Deut. 4:35; Isa. 43:10–13).

The True Birth of Jesus

Throughout the entire Bible, we will learn that God was known by many names, but first He existed only as the Holy Spirit, who could not be seen. Then He spoke the Lord into existence, who is His spiritual image, and then He was called the Lord God, because He was still the same God. In the Old Testament books, He was called by many names but mostly by the *Lord God* or the *Almighty God*. However, when we study the New Testament, we will learn that "The Lord Jesus" is the same "Lord" whom God spoke into existence in the beginning and in the process of time was commanded by the Heavenly Father to come into the world as "The Lord Jesus" to save us from sin. This is the same Lord Jesus who died on the cross like a common criminal, but God the Heavenly Father resurrected Him up from the dead on the third day. After Jesus's resurrection, He was seen by His apostles and many of His believers before He ascended back to the kingdom of heaven to sit at the right hand of the Heavenly Father (John 3:16–18; Matt. 28:16–20).

This book was written to help teach the understanding of the almighty power of God and His existence so that we can better understand His ways and His word. If we do not learn and understand the power of God, we will never understand the true Word of God.

Many of us know the story about the Virgin Mary, who was chosen by God to be the blessed vessel among women to spiritually conceive the Son of God, who is known to us as *Our Lord* and *Savior Jesus Christ*. Jesus is called the *Son of God* because He was spiritually placed into the belly of the Virgin Mary and was born covered in the likeness of human flesh. Jesus's flesh looked like ours and felt like ours, but His flesh was spiritual. Only spiritual beings can appear and disappear, walk on the water, change their outer look, and be transfigured (Luke 1:28–35).

Know also that not one drop of Mary's human blood entered the body of the Baby Jesus because only Mary's belly was isolated and used as the vessel to carry the Holy Child.

In Luke 1:35, God sent an angel to Mary with the message that she would be the woman to carry His Son, Jesus Christ. The angel said to her: "The Holy Ghost shall come upon you, and the power of the Highest shall overshadow you, and that Holy Thing which shall be born of you shall be called the Son of God." The Heavenly Father needed a way to send His Son into the world so that He would be accepted by humankind, and later His teachings and His spiritual proofs showed the world that He is the Son of God. Mary conceived Jesus in her belly by the Holy Spirit, and that was the same way that He was born; He entered her belly by the Spirit, and He was delivered out of her belly by the Holy Spirit. Yes, Mary had labor pains like all women in labor, but Jesus did not pass through Mary's womb. He came out of her belly by the Spirit, the same way that He was conceived in her belly. Therefore, no one was allowed to witness His birth, not even Joseph, Mary's husband, because that was one of the revelations of God that He decided would be revealed in these final days. Think about it, Mary was a virgin, engaged to be married; if the Baby Jesus, was allowed to pass through her womb, God would have robbed her and her husband of her virginity. Our God is a marvelous, magnificent God, and everything He does is done in righteousness. The Lord Jesus obeyed the commandment of God and came into the earth as the Son of God and the last prophet of God, and after He died for our sins, He went back to the kingdom of heaven to sit at the right hand of the Heavenly Father (Acts 2:32–33; 1 John 5:4–12).

CHAPTER 4

The Holy Trinity of God

There are some who do not understand or believe in what we call the *Holy Trinity of God* because they were never taught the true existence of God from the very beginning. The Holy Trinity, which consists of the one and only divine Spirit of God, consists of three divine persons which are the Father, the Son, and the Holy Ghost. May God open the eyes and understanding of the readers to receive the truth of His Holy Word in these final days. Amen.

God the Heavenly Father is the invisible Holy Spirit who existed alone before He spoke the Lord into existence by His powerful and almighty word (Matt. 6:9–13).

God the Son is the (Living Word) same Lord that God called into existence, to live in the kingdom of heaven, and the same Lord whom God sent into the world as the Baby Jesus to save us from our sins (John 3:34–36; Matt. 1:18–20).

God the Holy Ghost is a powerful anointing Spirit given by God to Jesus Christ, after He resurrected from the dead, to give to those whom He will empower to preach, teach, and do all the powerful miracles that He performed in His ministry while He was in the earth. Jesus told His apostles that the Holy Ghost will come into them and teach them everything that they need to know, because the unsaved world cannot teach them the true spiritual knowledge of God (1 John 2:27–28).

Some religious leaders and writers of today have eliminated the phrase *Holy Ghost* from their writings, teachings, and preaching and have replaced it with the phrase *Holy Spirit*. The Holy Spirit and the Holy Ghost are of the same Holy Spirit, but they each have a different purpose. The Holy Spirit is a saving spirit, which is given to us by God when we first become true believers, in our heart and mind. The second we become believers, we will receive a portion of God's Holy Spirit, which will instantly make us a child of God. Afterward, we must begin our spiritual relationship with God by reading, listening, studying, praying, and following His Holy Word. Being saved by the Holy Spirit is our personal reward and testimony for believing that Jesus Christ is the Son of God. With joy and happiness, we will share our testimony about our new birth with others to let them know we have given our life over to God. The evidence of being saved by the Holy Spirit is an inner joy and is only visual in our actions, our speech, and the changes in our lifestyle because we will go from worldly to godly in our heart and mind (John 3:16–18; John 7:39).

However, the Holy Ghost is a teaching Spirit with spiritual and physical evidence that can be seen and heard by others. When the apostles were filled with the Spirit of the Holy Ghost, they begin to speak in different languages that were not known to them. The purpose of the Holy Ghost allowing them to speak in these unknown tongues was to prove to others that they were not acting on their own, nor were they under the influence of any alcoholic beverage (Acts 2:1–21; 1 John 2:27; Mark 16:15–20; Acts 10:38–48; Acts 2:32–33).

In the New Testament, the anointing of the Holy Ghost came on His apostles on the day of Pentecost so that they could receive the spiritual power they needed to teach and continue Jesus's ministry (Acts 2:1–31).

God chose the apostles who followed Jesus during His ministry. They, too, were saved after they heard the teachings of Jesus and believed that He was truly the Son of God. However, they followed Jesus for about three years, but they did not receive the Holy Ghost until Jesus was crucified, arose from the dead, and went back to be with the Heavenly Father. Know this, God the Father gives the Holy Spirit, which saves us, with the promise of eternal life in the kingdom of heaven, and Jesus Christ gives the Holy Ghost, which teaches us and allows us to be His ministers. However, we do not need the Holy Ghost to enter the kingdom of heaven, because the Holy Ghost is not given to all believers. We enter the kingdom of heaven because we believed that Jesus is the Son of God, who was sent into the world to save us from our sins (John 3:16–21).

Again the Holy Trinity of God is of the same divine spirit that consists of three spiritual godheads for many different purposes. God is a God of love and power, and He can use anyone in any way He needs (John 14:12–14).

Understanding the Water Baptism

A one-time water baptism is a major step in the new life of the believer. The purpose of the water baptism is to wash away our past sins. These are the ungodly sins that we committed before we became believers and saved by the Holy Spirit of God. None of us can enter the kingdom of heaven without being forgiven for the sins that we had committed while we were living in this sinful world. On the day of judgment, the world will stand before God and answer for all the sins that we have done in our life. However, when we become believers and repent to God for our sins and receive the water baptism, our past sins will be forgiven, so our past record will be clean in the eyes of God. Now let us talk about our new sins that we will commit after we receive the water baptism. God did not create us perfect, and He knows that none of us will be perfect or sinless after we are saved. So God, in His infinite wisdom, power, and love, made a way for us to continue to be forgiven for our ungodly sins for the rest of our life, in this sinful and ungodly world. In His everlasting love for us, He has given us the spiritual gift of repentance. This spiritual gift allows us to continually ask and receive the forgiveness of our sins until the day we leave this world. As we are receiving the water baptism, He will bless us with the gift of repentance as we come up out of the water. Know that when we are baptized, we must be fully immersed in the water so that our whole body will be washed from head to toe and instantly forgiven for our past sins (Matt. 28:16–20; Luke 24:46–48; 1 John 5:4–12; Mark 1:4–11).

Most churches in accordance with the Holy Scriptures believe that we should be baptized in the name of the Holy Trinity, which is the Father, the Son, and the Holy Ghost. Our Lord and Savior Jesus Christ is a part of the Trinity, and it is He who has died on the cross so that we may have eternal life. Years ago, in the Holiness churches, the new believers were immersed completely in water as the preacher said these words: "My dear (sister or brother) I now baptize you in the name of the Father, the Son, and the Holy Ghost, and may you receive the Repentance of your sins and the Gift of the Holy Ghost. In Jesus Name" (Matt. 28:19–20).

Remember as saved believers, the gift of repentance will always be available to us whenever we fall short of the glory of God and sin. However, there is a warning that we must understand about our gift of repentance, which is this, we cannot purposely commit a sin and think that we will be forgiven. No, we will only be forgiven for our unintentional sins that we repent for. Remember, our God is a God who is all-knowing, all-power, and all-able to do all things. This is the short prayer that we continue to use to ask for forgiveness, which we can use for the rest of our life when we realize and recognize our unintentional sins: "Lord Jesus, I come to you confessing my sin, that I might receive the gift of repentance. In Jesus name I pray. Amen" (Matt. 3:11; Matt. 3:13–17; John 16:15–16).

CHAPTER 5

The Kingdom of Heaven Created

Let us review a little of our reading so far. Again, in the very existence before anything else existed, the Holy Spirit of God existed alone. Then He spoke the Lord into existence, whom He created in the image and likeness of Himself, then God, who cannot be seen, and His spiritual image, who can be seen by other spiritual beings. As the Lord God, He spoke the kingdom of heaven into existence, as a beautiful home for the Lord to reign as King of kings and Lord of all, but there was no one to rule over. So the Lord God, in His infinite wisdom and power of His Word, spoke into existence a tremendous number of angelic beings to fill up the kingdom of heaven. The purpose of these spiritual beings was to live in the kingdom and be ready to serve, honor, and obey the Lord God with all their heart, mind, and soul.

This heavenly host, better known as the angels of heaven, has no sexuality and no sexual desires, so they do not and have never engaged in any sexual activities in the kingdom of heaven or in the earth. These angels, like the Lord, were also created in the image and likeness of the heavenly Father, as was humankind, but the angels are made of spiritual flesh, and we, as human beings, were made from the dust of the ground. All living creatures were created with a different kind of flesh (Gen. 3:19; 1 Cor. 15:39–40).

After the kingdom of heaven was created and all that was needed in it, there was a time span of heavenly peace, but no one knows how long this time span lasted before the next event took place in the kingdom of heaven.

CHAPTER 6

The War in Heaven

After the time span of peace, we learned that there was a war in the kingdom of heaven among the angels. Each of these spiritual beings was created with various levels of spiritual powers, but some were much more powerful than others. Again these are individual beings just like us, with their own mind, body, and soul, but made of spiritual flesh. They were also given the gift of free will, to choose to obey or disobey, because God is not a dictating God who rules over our heart and mind. He allows us to make our own choices.

There was an angel living in the kingdom of heaven whose name was Lucifer, and the Bible tells us that he was an enormously powerful and popular angel, who was known as "the son of the morning." Lucifer was very well liked by the other angels, and he was more powerful than most of them, but he became so popular and self-centered that he eventually wanted to rule over the kingdom of heaven, in the place of the Lord God. The kingdom of heaven was usually a place of peace, so Lucifer had no idea how powerful the Lord and some of the other angels were, but he was convinced that he was powerful enough to take over the kingdom and rule as the highest (Isa. 14:12–14; Rev. 12:7–9).

What Lucifer did not know was, unlike him, the Lord was not given just a portion of God's spiritual power, because the Lord was made of God's spiritual power, which makes them one. Lucifer thought that he and the Lord were on the same spiritual level because they both were made in the same image and likeness as all the other spiritual beings. Unfortunately, in his lack of knowledge, Lucifer went about in the kingdom of heaven and convinced one-third of the heavenly angels to team up with him in a takeover.

Understand also that Lucifer did not have the power to create anything or anyone, nor did he own or control the angels that followed him into war. After he lost the war and was kicked out of the kingdom of heaven, his only desire was to steal, kill, and destroy everything that the Lord God had already created and made (John 10:10).

Lucifer's lack of knowledge proves that we are truly blessed because we have some knowledge that even the angels in heaven did not have.

Now there was another powerful angel living in the kingdom of heaven in this period, and his name was Michael. This angel was a spiritual warrior, known as the *Archangel,* and one who loved and obeyed the Lord God with all his heart, mind, soul, and strength. So Lucifer's attempt to take over the kingdom of heaven was not as easy as he may have thought it would be, because he had to fight against Michael the Archangel and all the other angels, who were still willing to serve and obey the Lord God. When the war was over, Lucifer and the fallen angels were totally defeated (Isa. 14:12–14).

Our Lord God is a powerful and loving God, who could have taken these fallen angels out of existence, but through His grace and mercy, He allowed them to live, and they were not given to Satan to use as he wishes (Jude 1:6).

CHAPTER 7

The Creation of the Earth

The Lord God did not participate in the war, but while the war was going on, He isolated a large space somewhere under the kingdom of heaven and surrounded it with a great amount of water. Soon after the war was over, the powerful but defeated angels and their leader, Lucifer, were kicked out of heaven and thrown into the empty space that was prepared for them, and the Lord God called the empty space *earth* (Rev. 12:7–17).

The Lord God knew how powerful He had created Lucifer and some of the other angels, so to keep them from coming up out of the empty earth and through the water, He surrounded the top of the water with His Holy Spirit. Remember none of the angels were anywhere near as powerful as the Lord God because the spirit of God is all-powerful, which meant that Lucifer and the other fallen angels were stuck down in the empty earth with no hope of coming out. Lucifer found out too late that he was not strong enough to break through the Holy Spirit of God and enter back into the kingdom of heaven.

This revelation informs us of the original purpose for the Lord God creating the earth, which was for a place for Lucifer and the other fallen angels who could no longer live in the kingdom of heaven after they had fallen into sin.

Think about it, those fallen angels were the first to live in the earth before the Lord God prepared it for humankind. Yes! We are living in the same earth today.

CHAPTER 8

The Creation of the Pit of Hell

Before the fallen angels were thrown into the empty earth, the earth on the inside was still filled with light because it was a part of the kingdom of heaven, and in this period before the war, no darkness existed. However, because these angels had sinned against God and lost every part of their righteousness, which was their Holy Spirit, their heavenly home, their angelic names, and their spiritual light, they were no longer angels of light but were now angels of darkness, and soon the earth on the inside was filled with their dark spirit.

This revelation informs us that God did not create darkness because God is the Spirit of light and life, and there is no darkness in Him (1 John 1:5).

The darkness was automatically created when the angels lost their righteousness and their Holy Spirit; we know that the absence of light is dark, and the opposite of dark is light.

However, God allowed the darkness to exist in the earth as a part of their everlasting punishment for disobeying Him and trying to overtake the kingdom of heaven. Again our God is all-knowing, all-powerful, and all-able to do anything but fail, and He always has a plan of His own because He also knows the future.

At this time, Lucifer's godly name was changed to the ungodly name of *Satan* because he was their leader and the most powerful one among the fallen angels, so he became a powerful evil force, who learned a hard lesson when he thought that he was powerful enough to go against the Almighty God.

However, God did not strip the angels of their individual powers that were given to them when they were created, which was why He surrounded the earth with great waters and a layer of His Holy Spirit. God knew that they would forever try to escape out the dark empty earth, and their constant struggle will also be a part of their punishment.

This revelation lets us know that the earth was first used as a dark empty prison for the fallen angels, and when the Lord God decided to use the same earth to create a home for mankind, He spoke into the darkness and said: "Let there be light." The darkness along with the fallen angels was sent all the way down to the bottom of the earth, and God sealed it close again with His Holy Spirit. This meant that the fallen angels were now down in a dark pit under the earth, known to us now as the *pit of hell*.

The Bible also tells us that all these angels who followed Satan instead of God will remain down in the pit of hell in spiritual chains until the day of judgment (Jude 1:6).

The Prayer for Salvation

After you have read this book and you feel in your heart and mind that you are in need of the salvation of God, please say this Spirit-filled prayer to ask God to come into your life and fill you with His Holy Spirit.

> Heavenly Father, I know that I am a sinner in need of your salvation. I believe, Jesus Christ is Your Son, whom you sent into the world to die for my sins. I am now asking you to come into my heart and fill me with your Holy

Spirit so that Imay be able to live an eternal life in your kingdom of heaven. Amen. (John 3:16–18; John 14:6; Acts 16:30)

ABOUT THE AUTHOR

First and foremost, I, Minister Johnson, would like to thank everyone for purchasing and taking the time to read this book. The teachings and spiritual revelations written were revealed to me by the Holy Spirit. Who I am and my personal life is not important, because I was just a used vessel to write the words of God that were given to me to write.

At a very young age, I became curious about God and who He was. However, at the beginning stage of my curiosity, I was too young to read and understand the words of the Holy Bible, but I would take time and admire the beautiful colored pictures in our big family Bible. We were a church-going family, so I often heard about how great God was and how He sent His only begotten Son into the world to save us from our sins. When I got older, I became a Bible scholar and a minister of the Word of God. Studying and teaching the Bible down through the years have been a blessing in my life. I pray that this book will give its readers a better understanding of some of the events that took place in the world "before the existence of mankind." Thank you and God bless.